*Wild Ducks.* To me, these two words are synonymous. Indeed, ducks' very wildness makes them unfamiliar to many people. Most of us recognize the widespread mallard and colorful wood duck, but in this collection you will also come face to face with less familiar species such as the diminutive bufflehead, the graceful pintail, and the regal canvasback.

Although varied in color, size, and pattern, all ducks share a dependence on watery habitat for nesting, and sadly, they often prefer areas that we humans find attractive for agriculture and other development. Drought conditions in many areas have further complicated things for waterfowl, and declining numbers of the redhead and other species have brought them close to threatened status.

But waterfowl are resilient birds. With a few breaks from civilization and the weather, their numbers can recover. I hope this collection gives you an awareness of what we lose every time a marsh is drained or a river polluted. Ducks deserve our help for the beauty they give, the habitat they symbolize, and the wilderness they embody.

Dr. Scott Nielsen is an avian taxidermist and photographer specializing in waterfowl and birds of prey. He holds degrees and advanced training from the University of Wisconsin, University of Arizona, and Northwestern University. While at Northwestern, he studied under Leon Pray at the Field Museum of Natural History and was able to prepare many of the world's rarest birds, including remounting specimens of the now extinct Labrador duck and passenger pigeon. Since 1968, Nielsen's studio has been located near the historic portage between the St. Croix and Brule rivers in northwestern Wisconsin. His photography has appeared in virtually every North American outdoor and nature publication, plus numerous calendars, posters, books, and sportswear products.

Since 1988, Nielsen has been the contract photographer for Ducks Unlimited, an international organization dedicated to preserving and restoring the world's wetlands and their associated wildlife. His latest books are *A Season with Eagles* and *Songbirds Postcard Collection,* also published by Voyageur Press.

# Wild Ducks Postcard Collection

**Scott Nielsen**

**Voyageur Press**

Copyright © 1991 by Scott Nielsen

All rights reserved. No part of this work may be reproduced or used in any form by any means—graphic, electronic, or mechanical, including photocopying, recording, taping, or any information storage and retrieval system—without written permission of the publisher.

Printed in Hong Kong through Bookbuilders Ltd.
91 92 93 94 95 5 4 3 2 1

ISBN 0-89658-165-9

Published by
Voyageur Press, Inc.
P.O. Box 338
123 North Second Street
Stillwater, MN 55082 U.S.A.
From Minnesota and Canada 612-430-2210
Toll-free 800-888-9653

Voyageur Press books are also available at discounts for quantities for educational, fundraising, premium, or sales-promotion use. For details contact the marketing department. Please write or call for our free catalog of natural history publications.

Pintail *(Anas acuta)*

From the *Wild Ducks Postcard Collection.* Copyright © 1991 by Scott Nielsen. Voyageur Press, 123 N. 2nd St., Stillwater, MN 55082 USA

Ruddy Duck *(Oxyura jamaicensis)*

From the *Wild Ducks Postcard Collection.* Copyright © 1991 by Scott Nielsen. Voyageur Press, 123 N. 2nd St., Stillwater, MN 55082 USA

Fulvous Whistling-Duck *(Dendrocygna bicolor)*

From the *Wild Ducks Postcard Collection.* Copyright © 1991 by Scott Nielsen. Voyageur Press, 123 N. 2nd St., Stillwater, MN 55082 USA

Wood Duck *(Aix sponsa)*

From the *Wild Ducks Postcard Collection*. Copyright © 1991 by Scott Nielsen. Voyageur Press, 123 N. 2nd St., Stillwater, MN 55082 USA

Gadwall *(Anas strepera)*

From the *Wild Ducks Postcard Collection.* Copyright © 1991 by Scott Nielsen. Voyageur Press, 123 N. 2nd St., Stillwater, MN 55082 USA

Mallard *(Anas platyrhynchos)*

From the *Wild Ducks Postcard Collection.* Copyright © 1991 by Scott Nielsen. Voyageur Press, 123 N. 2nd St., Stillwater, MN 55082 USA

Common Eider *(Somateria mollissima)*

From the *Wild Ducks Postcard Collection.* Copyright © 1991 by Scott Nielsen. Voyageur Press, 123 N. 2nd St., Stillwater, MN 55082 USA

Cinnamon Teal *(Anas cyanoptera)*

From the *Wild Ducks Postcard Collection.* Copyright © 1991 by Scott Nielsen. Voyageur Press, 123 N. 2nd St., Stillwater, MN 55082 USA

Baikal Teal *(Anas formosa)*

From the *Wild Ducks Postcard Collection*. Copyright © 1991 by Scott Nielsen. Voyageur Press, 123 N. 2nd St., Stillwater, MN 55082 USA

Northern Shoveler *(Anas clypeata)*

From the *Wild Ducks Postcard Collection*. Copyright © 1991 by Scott Nielsen. Voyageur Press, 123 N. 2nd St., Stillwater, MN 55082 USA

**Bufflehead** *(Bucephala albeola)*

From the *Wild Ducks Postcard Collection.* Copyright © 1991 by Scott Nielsen. Voyageur Press, 123 N. 2nd St., Stillwater, MN 55082 USA

Lesser Scaup *(Aythya affinis)*

From the *Wild Ducks Postcard Collection.* Copyright © 1991 by Scott Nielsen. Voyageur Press, 123 N. 2nd St., Stillwater, MN 55082 USA

Hooded Merganser *(Lophodytes cucullatus)*

From the *Wild Ducks Postcard Collection*. Copyright © 1991 by Scott Nielsen. Voyageur Press, 123 N. 2nd St., Stillwater, MN 55082 USA

Common Merganser *(Mergus merganser)*

From the *Wild Ducks Postcard Collection.* Copyright © 1991 by Scott Nielsen. Voyageur Press, 123 N. 2nd St., Stillwater, MN 55082 USA

American Wigeon *(Anas americana)*

From the *Wild Ducks Postcard Collection*. Copyright © 1991 by Scott Nielsen. Voyageur Press, 123 N. 2nd St., Stillwater, MN 55082 USA

Ring-necked Duck *(Aythya collaris)*

From the *Wild Ducks Postcard Collection.* Copyright © 1991 by Scott Nielsen. Voyageur Press, 123 N. 2nd St., Stillwater, MN 55082 USA

Canvasback *(Aythya valisineria)*

From the *Wild Ducks Postcard Collection.* Copyright © 1991 by Scott Nielsen. Voyageur Press, 123 N. 2nd St., Stillwater, MN 55082 USA

Redhead *(Aythya americana)*

From the *Wild Ducks Postcard Collection.* Copyright © 1991 by Scott Nielsen. Voyageur Press, 123 N. 2nd St., Stillwater, MN 55082 USA

Blue-winged Teal *(Anas discors)*

From the *Wild Ducks Postcard Collection.* Copyright © 1991 by Scott Nielsen. Voyageur Press, 123 N. 2nd St., Stillwater, MN 55082 USA